The Pintele Haggadah

The Pintele Haggadah

פינטעלע הגדה של פסח

NOAH DIAMOND

The Pintele Haggadah

Seriously, though, if you want to make copies for private seder use, go ahead, have a good time! Maybe you'll consider buying at least a few, though, to help keep a roof over the author's head...?

FIRST EDITION

ISBN 979-8-218-90689-4

Book design and illustrations by the author.

This typeface is Baskervald, created by Arkandis Digital Foundry.

noahdiamond.com

Printed in the United States of America

For Aunt Sarah and Uncle Joe

Dayenu

pintele yid

(PIN-teh-leh YIHD)

n. Essential Jewishness; the essence of a Jew. "A lot of sentimental stories of the *shtetl* deal with the *pintele yid.*" *Origin:* Yiddish. *Etymology:* **דאָס פּינטעלע ייִד** *dos píntele yíd.* *lit.* "the dot of the Jew; the quintessence of one's Jewish identity."

— Jewish English Lexicon

CONTENTS

INTRODUCTION

he Pintele Haggadah came into being as a result of my audio series *Pintele*, an exploration of Jewish identity. (You can learn more about *Pintele*, and listen to all seven chapters of the series, at noahdiamond.com/pintele.)

In the *Pintele* series, I discover that in middle age, it's become important to me to revisit some of the Jewish traditions of my childhood, despite the fact that I'm a nonreligious nonbeliever. This Haggadah is a product of that desire to uphold Jewish traditions, moderated by the need to uphold them in a way that works for me.

I stopped celebrating Passover many years ago. Partly, this was due to a general rejection of religion. But then there was the Exodus from Egypt, also known as *the story of Passover* — a powerful story, but a mythological one. Despite deep skepticism about the Bible, I had always assumed that there was sound historical basis for the general idea that the ancient Hebrews were slaves in Egypt, and it broke my heart to learn that there wasn't. (This is explored in detail in Part Three of the *Pintele* audio series.)

Working on *Pintele* helped me realize that the myths of God and Egypt are not as central to Passover as they may seem. At its heart, Passover is a celebration of liberation. It provides the poetic and philosophical framework for the Jewish imperative to oppose tyrants and be allies of the oppressed. Mythology notwithstanding, it's supremely admirable that for thousands of years Jewish people have held an annual festival that celebrates the liberation of enslaved people and the downfall of fascists! Celebrating these things is at the heart of what it means to be Jewish, god or no god. Too many of our Jewish ancestors have suffered and died for us to drop the ball now.

Although the story of ancient Israelites enslaved by an unspecified Egyptian Pharaoh is a work of fiction, the traditional Haggadah is still profoundly correct when it says that *In every generation they rise against us and seek our destruction.* Indeed, Jewish history is a long series of golden ages cut short by persecution, segregation, deportation, and execution. Passover, a Jewish antifascist festival celebrating freedom, has plenty of *real* history to draw from. We don't have to pad our résumé when it comes to being persecuted — or to overcoming persecution, and helping others to overcome it. Fighting tyranny is a Jewish tradition.

The goal of *The Pintele Haggadah* is to avoid some old errors, while preserving the beauty, power, and meaning of the seders I remember from childhood. These pages include a sprinkling of irreverent humor, because my family's seders did, and I think Passover should be fun. I hope you find that I've hit the right notes, but if the changes I've made are not the changes *you* would make, I encourage you to do what I've done, and adapt the Haggadah to your own standards. I've left plenty of empty space in the margins, as well as some blank pages at the end, so you can use this as a workbook for designing your own seder.

Those childhood Passovers were always led by my great uncle, Joe Brody. The main source for Uncle Joe's seder was the hugely popular Rabbi Nathan Goldberg Haggadah, published in the United States by Ktav Publishing House — the one with the red and yellow paper cover, usually blotted with decades of Manischewitz wine stains.

But Uncle Joe's intense preparations involved poring over several other Haggadahs too, with a range of styles and approaches, circling passages and incorporating them into our seder. At every place setting, along with a weathered copy of the Goldberg, there would be several pages of supplementary material, gathered from a variety of sources. The idea that families can create their own seders in this way strikes me as just the right mix of tradition and progress. I hope that even *some* of *The Pintele Haggadah* finds a place at your Passover table.

With that approach in mind, I've felt free to dispense with a good deal of what one expects to find in a Haggadah. If you'd like to include the parting of the Red Sea, surely you know where to find it. (It's right between Asia and Africa.)

In these pages, most of the seder is presented in a call-and-response format, with the "LEADER" reading the main narration aloud and the "GROUP" responding in unison. Some sections are marked "READ AROUND THE TABLE," with the intention that all participants in the seder will take turns reading short passages. But these assignments are just suggestions, and the text should work however you assign it. You may prefer a seder with no leader, in which the "READ AROUND THE TABLE" approach is applied to all of the passages marked "LEADER"; or you may choose to have multiple leaders.

Seders are educational, and especially if children are participating, it's a good practice to stop periodically to ask and answer questions; and to explain and discuss challenging words and ideas as they arise. The real content of a good seder is not just the text in the Haggadah, but the conversation that takes place at the table.

Despite the absence of a god in these pages (and in the universe), some traditional Hebrew prayers (with English transliteration and translation) are included, so you can incorporate them into your seder if you want to. I don't think we have to believe in a literal god to find power in these ancient sounds, or in the idea that Jewish people have said these words for thousands of years. Believers who are confident in their beliefs needn't be offended when nonbelievers express spiritual doubt; nonbelievers likewise need not feel affronted by the sound of prayer.

The Pintele Haggadah is intended for pratical use. I want it to be a slender volume that can sit at every place setting, and can be reasonably gotten through in the course of an evening, with plenty of time left to talk. If you're interested in a detailed account of the Passovers I remember from my childhood, and of my evolving feelings about the holiday, I refer you to Part Three of the *Pintele* audio series. Jewish atheism is explored in Part Two; a humanistic approach to Judaism is discussed in Part Seven. The entire series is filled with material which may be of interest to readers of this Haggadah.

Please feel free to make copies of this as needed (but please, for private, free distribution only). I don't expect you to buy thirty copies if you're having thirty people over for Passover. But I *would* appreciate it if you'd purchase at least *some* published copies, because they're nice, and it'll help keep a roof over this author's head.

Thank you for opening *The Pintele Haggadah.*

Happy Passover!

Noah

Noah Diamond
New York City
2026

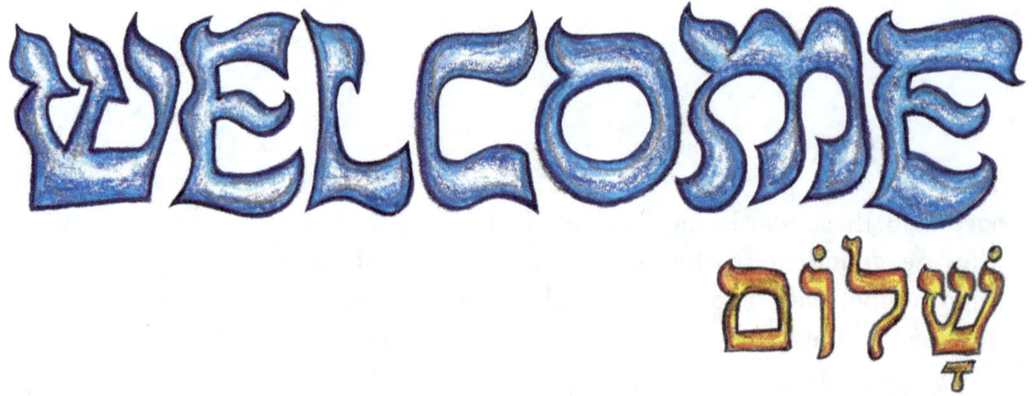

LEADER GROUP

Old friends, new friends, family, and neighbors...

Welcome to our Passover seder.

Passover is a celebration of liberation,
a festival of freedom.

Let all who are hungry come and eat.

We know we are lucky to be together.

We know we are lucky to be free.

While we celebrate tonight, we light candles
to acknowledge all those we love
who are not here with us,
and all those in the world
who still suffer at the hands of tyrants.

LEADER

When our ancestors lit candles,
they would say a prayer in Hebrew.

בָּרוּךְ אַתָּה יְיָ	*Barukh atah adonai*
אֱלֹהֵינוּ מֶלֶךְ הָעוֹלָם	*eloheinu, melekh ha'olam*
אֲשֶׁר קִדְּשָׁנוּ בְּמִצְוֹתָיו	*asher kid'shanu b'mitzvotav*
וְצִוָּנוּ לְהַדְלִיק נֵר	*v'tzivanu l'hadlik neir*
שֶׁל פֶּסַח	*shel pesach*

ENGLISH TRANSLATION:

Blessed are you, lord our god, king of the universe,
who has sanctified us with his commandments
and commanded us to light the lights of Passover.

LEADER

At our seder tonight, we thank one another —
for the time and effort to be here together,
to prepare this meal and this celebration.

(The Leader may insert specific thanks here to the hosts, to those who have prepared the meal, and to anyone else who might be acknowledged.

(This could be a time to "go around the table" and have each participant express thanks for something meaningful about the occasion.)

And so, we light candles and we give thanks.

GROUP

Thank you,
old friends, new friends,
family, and neighbors,
for being here with us tonight
to celebrate our freedom,
and to light the candles
which represent our wish
for freedom for all people.

(Candles are lit.)

THE FIRST CUP

LEADER GROUP

And now, shall we have a little something?

Yes, let's have a little something.

In a traditional seder, each participant
drinks four cups of wine or grape juice,
which are poured at specific times
and prayed over in Hebrew.
At our seder tonight, you can have
four cups of whatever you like,
and pray or not pray, as you wish.

TRADITIONAL PRAYER IN HEBREW:

בָּרוּךְ אַתָּה יְיָ	*Barukh atah adonai*
אֱלֹהֵינוּ מֶלֶךְ הָעוֹלָם	*eloheinu, melekh ha'olam*
בּוֹרֵא פְּרִי הַגָּפֶן:	*borei p'ri hagafen*

ENGLISH TRANSLATION:

Blessed are you, lord our god, king of the universe, who creates the fruit of the vine

LEADER GROUP

We remember to share what we have.

We thank the people whose labor brought these refreshments to our table.

(The first cup is poured and enjoyed.)

THE SEDER PLATE

LEADER		GROUP
This is the seder plate.	
	Very nice, very nice.

PARSLEY

EGG
(traditionally this would be a roasted egg; the best way to roast an egg is to boil it first)

GREEN VEGETABLE
(lettuce)

CHAROSET
(a chunky paste made of apples, nuts, and wine or grape juice; a little cinnamon and honey couldn't hurt)

BITTER HERB
(horseradish)

A SHANK BONE *is traditional, because of the role a slaughtered lamb plays in the traditional Passover myth. But who wants to look at a shank bone? For that matter, who wants to slaughter a lamb? My mother would use a little lamb she made out of clay; that was cute. Just put something nice here.*

Parsley and Salt Water

LEADER | GROUP

This is parsley.
It represents the springtime harvest.

And the goodness of the earth.

This is salt water.
It represents the tears of our ancestors.

And the suffering of all oppressed people.

We now eat parsley dipped in salt water,
to remind us that we are lucky to be
eating and celebrating together.

We are grateful to our parents,
to our grandparents,
and to all the generations
who came before us.

We honor them by remembering their words,
their struggles, and their triumphs;
and by treating one another
with kindness, patience, and generosity.

We honor their laughter.
We honor their tears.

(Everyone eats parsley dipped in salt water.)

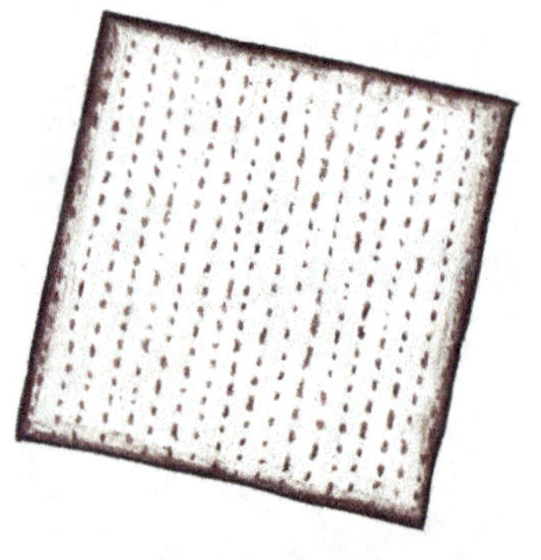

(The Leader uncovers three matzos and holds up the middle matzo.)

LEADER — GROUP

This is matzo, the bread of affliction.

This is matzo, the bread of affliction.

I just said that.

I just said that.

Now cut that out!

Now cut that out!

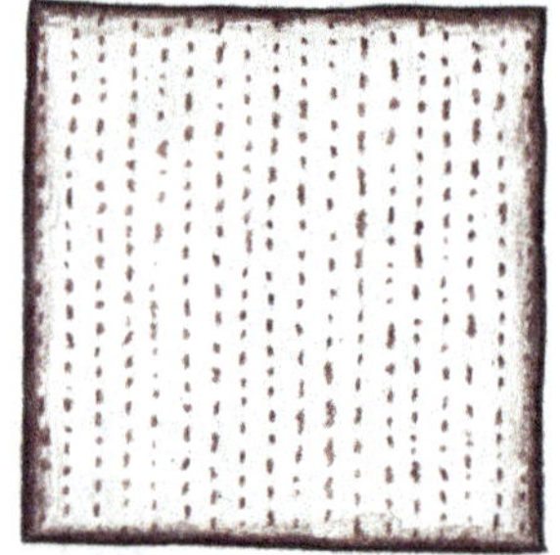

According to the Exodus myth,
when our ancestors escaped from slavery
they didn't have time to make bread for their journey.
So instead of waiting for the dough to rise,
they ate unleavened bread.

It's like a cracker.

We eat matzo to remind us to stay flexible
and spontaneous, to make do with what we have,
and to act quickly when circumstance demands it.

Matzo. The official bread of being in a hurry.

Now I'm going to take a piece of this middle matzo,
and during the meal I'm going to hide it somewhere.
After the meal you can look for it,
and whoever finds it gets a prize or something.
This is known as the *afikomen.*
Afikomen means *dessert* in Hebrew.
But don't worry, we'll have a nice desert too.

You know, they also have
chocolate-covered matzo.
It's available wherever matzo is sold.

(Matzo is distributed to everyone at the table.)

TRADITIONAL PRAYER IN HEBREW:

בָּרוּךְ אַתָּה יְיָ
אֱלֹהֵינוּ מֶלֶךְ הָעוֹלָם
הַמּוֹצִיא לֶחֶם
מִן הָאָרֶץ

Barukh atah adonai
eloheinu, melekh ha'olam
hamotzi lechem
min haaretz

ENGLISH TRANSLATION:

Blessed are you, lord our god, king of the universe,
who brings forth bread from the earth.

TRADITIONAL PRAYER IN HEBREW:

בָּרוּךְ אַתָּה יְיָ
אֱלֹהֵינוּ מֶלֶךְ הָעוֹלָם
וְצִוָּנוּ, עַל אֲכִילַת מַצָּה
אֲשֶׁר קִדְּשָׁנוּ, בְּמִצְוֹתָיו

Barukh atah adonai
eloheinu, melekh ha'olam
asher kid'shanu b'mitzvotav
v'tzivanu al achilat matzo

ENGLISH TRANSLATION:

Blessed are you, lord our god, king of the universe,
who hallows us with mitzvot, commanding us
regarding the eating of matzo.

GREEN VEGETABLE

LEADER | GROUP

Next we have a green vegetable.

But we just had some parsley.

That was different; that was to dip in the salt water.

Okay. We apologize. Please continue.

This green vegetable represents the springtime harvest.

You said the same thing about the parsley.

Don't be a noodge. Take some and let's move on.

(Everyone takes some lettuce.)

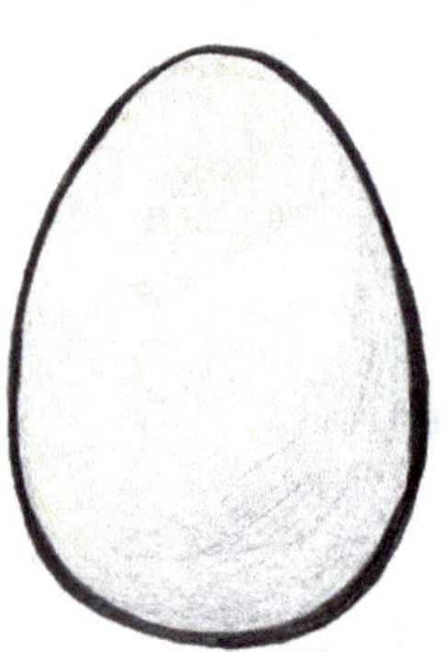

The next item on our seder plate is an egg.

We thank the chickens for all they have given us.

The egg represents new life.

And the promise of breakfast.

(Everyone takes some egg.)

LEADER

GROUP

This is *charoset*,
made with apples, nuts,
and wine or grape juice.

And a little cinnamon and honey couldn't hurt.

Charoset means *clay* in Hebrew.
It represents the clay used by enslaved people
subjected to forced labor.

*To make buildings
they were not permitted to enter.*

We eat *charoset*
to remind us of the importance
of autonomy, fair compensation,
and dignity for all workers everywhere.

(Everyone takes some charoset.)

BITTER HERBS AND THE HILLEL SUPREME

LEADER GROUP

Next, we have a bitter herb, such as horseradish.

It's okay. We like horseradish.

To remind us of the bitterness of slavery.

And the pain of oppression.

Over two thousand years ago, there was a Jewish scholar and teacher named Hillel. He said many wise things.

*"If I am not for myself, who will be for me?
And being for myself, what am I?
And if not now, when?"*

That was a good one.

"That which is hateful to you, do not do unto others."

Hillel began the tradition of eating matzo and bitter herbs together, in what became known as the Hillel sandwich.

Hillel was the first Jewish celebrity to have a sandwich named after him.

LEADER

GROUP

Tonight, we expand upon the tradition of the Hillel sandwich by eating lettuce, egg, charoset, and bitter herbs together on matzo.

The Hillel Supreme.

(Everyone eats the sandwich.)

HILLEL AT THE CARNEGIE DELI

THE SECOND CUP

LEADER — GROUP

And now, let us enjoy the second cup of wine, or juice, or whatever we prefer.

That does sound enjoyable.

And let's talk about the meaning of Passover.

That, too, sounds enjoyable.

READ AROUND THE TABLE

The traditional Haggadah tells a mythological story from the Torah (or Bible), in which the ancient Hebrews are enslaved by an evil ruler of Egypt. They're freed from slavery by Moses, assisted by a powerful god. This is known as the Exodus story.

Even though the Exodus story is not true, there is truth in the story's message, about the evil of tyranny, the value of freedom, and the power of hope.

Although the ancient Hebrews were not slaves in Egypt, the traditional Haggadah is not wrong when it says that Jewish people have been the victims of totalitarian oppression throughout history.

The traditional Haggadah says, "In every generation, they rise against us and seek our destruction."

The Assyrian conquest of Israel, around 2,750 years ago, forcibly relocated tens of thousands of Israelites. Whatever was left fell in the Babylonian siege of Jerusalem about 130 years later, which began the Babylonian captivity of the Jews.

Throughout history, there have been Golden Ages when Jewish people were free and thriving, followed by long periods of oppression.

There was a nice little period around the 160s BCE, after the Maccabean Revolt, which is celebrated during Hanukkah. This was followed by centuries of being persecuted by the Romans.

There was a brilliant Jewish golden age in fifteenth-century Spain, prior to the deportation or torture and murder of Jewish people during the Spanish Inquisition.

In the nineteenth and twentieth centuries, Jewish people living in Eastern Europe were oppressed by the Russian government and its armies of Cossacks.

During the Second World War, six million Jewish people were murdered by the Nazis in Europe.

And of course, many other groups of people, besides Jews, have been persecuted by tyrannical leaders and their followers, throughout history.

Here in the United States, between five and ten million people from Africa, and their descendants, were enslaved before slavery was abolished in 1865.

Today, all over the world, millions of people are enslaved, or suffering, or living in fear and desperation, due to the greed and cruelty of tyrants.

Because of our long history as subjects of oppression, Jewish people must always be allies of oppressed people everywhere.

GROUP

Our seder
is a celebration
of humanity's ongoing
exodus from persecution.

In solidarity with the entire human race,
we celebrate the glory of freedom
and renew our promise to help
build a better and freer world.

We pledge kindness, patience,
generosity, and honesty
to one another
and to all people
everywhere.

FOUR QUESTIONS

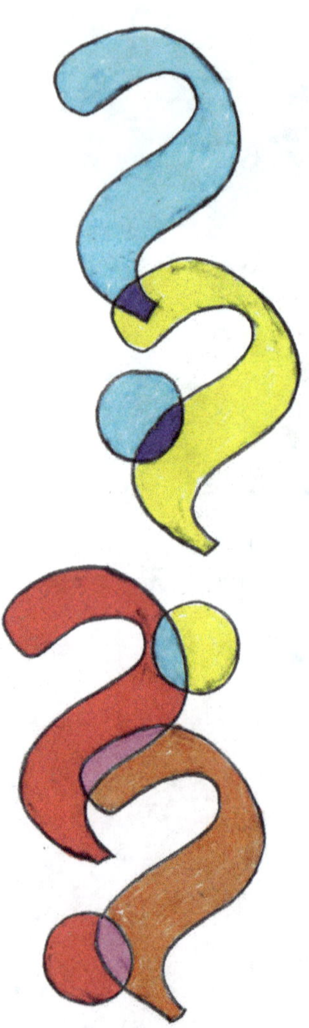

LEADER | GROUP

In a traditional seder,
the youngest person at the table asks
four specific questions, which are
organized around one big question.

Why is this night different from all other nights?

That is the big question.
Then, the traditional four questions
ask about the meaning of matzo, salt water,
and bitter herbs, and the tradition of reclining
comfortably at the seder table.

We've already covered that stuff.

Yes, but we can still sing the song if you want to.

It's up to you.

In 1936, the four questions in Hebrew
were set to music by the composer Ephraim Abileah.
That version has been sung by Jewish children
at seder tables ever since.

מַה־נִּשְׁתַּנָּה הַלַּיְלָה הַזֶּה מִכָּל־הַלֵּילוֹת

Why is this night different from all other nights?

Mah nishtanah, ha-laylah ha-zeh,
mi-kol ha-leylot, mi-kol ha-leylot,
ha-laylah ha-zeh, ha-laylah ha-zeh,
mi-kol ha-leylot,
ha-laylah ha-zeh, ha-laylah ha-zeh,
mi-kol ha-leylot?

שֶׁבְּכָל־הַלֵּילוֹת אָנוּ אוֹכְלִין חָמֵץ וּמַצָּה הַלַּיְלָה הַזֶּה כֻּלּוֹ מַצָּה

On all other nights, we eat leavened bread. Why on this night do we matzo?

She-b'khol ha-leylot 'anu 'okhlin
chameytz u-matzah, chameytz u-matzah,
ha-laylah ha-zeh, ha-laylah ha-zeh,
kulo matzah,
ha-laylah ha-zeh, ha-laylah ha-zeh,
kulo matzah?

שֶׁבְּכָל־הַלֵּילוֹת אָנוּ אוֹכְלִין שְׁאָר יְרָקוֹת הַלַּיְלָה הַזֶּה מָרוֹר

On all other nights, we eat all kinds of vegetables. Why on this night do we eat bitter herbs?

She-b'khol ha-leylot 'anu 'okhlin
sh'ar y'rakot, sh'ar y'rakot,
ha-laylah ha-zeh, ha-laylah ha-zeh,
maror, maror,
ha-laylah ha-zeh, ha-laylah ha-zeh,
maror, maror?

שֶׁבְּכָל־הַלֵּילוֹת אֵין אָנ
ו מַטְבִּילִין אֲפִלּוּ פַּעַם אֶחָת
הַלַּיְלָה הַזֶּה, שְׁתֵּי פְעָמִים

On all other nights, we don't dip even once. Why on this night do we dip twice?

She-b'khol ha-leylot 'eyn 'anu matbilin
'afilu pa'am 'achat, 'afilu pa'am 'achat,
ha-laylah ha-zeh, ha-laylah ha-zeh,
shtey p'amim,
ha-laylah ha-zeh, ha-laylah ha-zeh,
shtey p'amim?

שֶׁבְּכָל־הַלֵּילוֹת אָנוּ אוֹכְלִין בֵּין יוֹשְׁבִין וּבֵין מְסֻבִּין הַלַּיְלָה הַזֶּה כֻּלָּנוּ מְסֻבִּין

On all other nights, we eat either sitting upright or reclining. Why on this night do we recline?

She-b'khol ha-leylot 'anu 'okhlin
beyn yoshvin u-veyn m'subin,
beyn yoshvin u-veyn m'subin,
ha-laylah ha-zeh, ha-laylah ha-zeh,
kulanu m'subin,
ha-laylah ha-zeh, ha-laylah ha-zeh,
kulanu m'subin?

MORE QUESTIONS

LEADER

Traditional Jewish practice encourages
its followers to ask questions.
And so, in that spirit of open inquiry,
we set aside this time to ask each other questions,
and to answer each other's questions.

It can be about anything:
You can ask about the seder, about personal history,
about whether you've seen any good movies lately.
It can be a "what do you think?" question
or a "what's your favorite?" question
or any kind of question.

I'll begin.

(The leader may begin by asking a question to the person on their right, who then asks a question to the person on their right, and so on, going around the table. In larger groups, perhaps those with questions raise their hands to be called on, and ask whomever they wish. Manage this conversation in whatever way is best for the people at your seder.

(On the next page are some examples of questions, or kinds of questions, that might be asked, and some space to note new questions. Having the "right" questions or answers isn't important here. What matters is that we feel free to ask questions, that we try to answer each other's questions honestly, and listen carefully to each other's questions and answers.)

GENERAL QUESTIONS

What does it mean to be free?

What is the value of tradition?

Would you rather live today, or in a previous era?

Would you rather be younger or older?

Do you find it easier to talk or to listen?

What are you most frightened of?

What do you most look forward to?

How important is luck?

What is love?

PERSONAL QUESTIONS

What is your earliest memory?

What's changed the most in your lifetime?

What would you like to change about yourself, but can't?

What would you like to change about yourself, and could?

What's one thing you'd like to change about someone else?

What book / film / record / other work of art would you take to a desert island?

Do you believe in the existence of a god?

QUESTIONS RELIGION ATTEMPTS TO ANSWER

Why are we here?

How did we get to be here?

What makes us human?

What happens after we die?

EVEN MORE QUESTIONS

TEN PLAGUES עֶשֶׂר הַמַּכּוֹת

READ AROUND THE TABLE

Let us pour the third cup and consider the Ten Plagues.

The traditional Haggadah includes the myth of the Ten Plagues — ten terrible things that happen to the evil Pharaoh who enslaves the ancient Hebrews in the story.

The river turns to blood, or the land is infested with locusts, each time Moses says "Let my people go" and the Pharaoh refuses.

In the traditional seder, the Ten Plagues are recited, and wine is spilled from each glass as each plague is mentioned, in an expression of sympathy for the innocent victims of the plagues.

Tonight, we focus on ten plagues of our time.

As we recite these ten plagues together, using fingers or spoons to spill some wine on our plates, let's think of all we can do to oppose and vanquish these plagues, in ourselves and in the world around us.

(This list of plagues may be revised as preferred by the guests at your seder.

(If there are children present - or even if there aren't - this recitation of plagues may be followed by a discussion, in which words are defined, meanings discussed, and questions asked and answered.

(The explanations at the bottom of the next page may be used for further discussion.)

GREED

RACISM

SEXISM

HOMO- & TRANSPHOBIA

VIOLENCE

NATIONALISM

THEOCRACY

SCAPEGOATING

DEMAGOGUERY

DEHUMANIZATION

Greed is the incessant, selfish desire for more than is needed, at the expense of others.

Racism is prejudice on the basis of a marginalized racial or ethnic identity.

Sexism is prejudice on the basis of sex or gender.

Homophobia and ***transphobia*** are prejudices on the basis of sexual orientation or transgender identity.

Violence is the use of physical force with the intention to hurt, damage, or kill.

Nationalism is the glorification of one country or national interest at the expense of others.

Theocracy is the intrusion of religion on laws and government.

Scapegoating is the blaming of personal or societal problems on a marginalized group.

Demagoguery is political activity that exploits desires and prejudice over law, fact, or reason.

Dehumanization is treating or characterizing a group of people as less than human.

THE MEAL

LEADER GROUP

And now,
let's set the book aside
and enjoy a festive meal.

It's about time.

We'll continue with our seder
after we eat.

Please pass the salt.

(Eat!)

MATZO BALL
(KNEIDL)
SOUP

THE FOURTH CUP
AND THE ELIJAH-MIRIAM CUP

LEADER GROUP

Now that we've enjoyed a festive meal,
we reconvene for Act Two of our Passover seder.

Don't worry. It's short!

Let us now pour and enjoy the fourth cup!
Wine, juice, coffee, seltzer,
a half teaspoon of baking soda
in four ounces of water — whatever you like.

READ AROUND THE TABLE

As we enjoy the fourth cup of whatever we're drinking, let's take a moment to fill an extra cup for another guest.

The traditional Haggadah suggests leaving a cup of wine on the table for Elijah the Prophet, a mythological character from the Torah who functions as a wise man and problem solver.

Some more modern Haggadahs suggest also including a cup of water in honor of another Biblical character, Miriam, sister of Moses.

Tonight, we pratice a new tradition by filling the Elijah-Miriam cup in honor of all our heroes — the people we admire, respect, and look to for guidance and inspiration.

Let's go around the table and name them.

(Discuss.)

PASSOVER, 1943

This is adapted from several versions of the "Passover, 1943" section which has appeared in many family Haggadahs since around 1975. Its original authorship is unknown.

READ AROUND THE TABLE

The date that the Nazis chose to destroy the Warsaw Ghetto was Passover, April 19, 1943.

By this time, the Jews of the Ghetto knew that the daily trains to Treblinka were not transporting anyone to resettlement camps, but were taking them to be killed in the gas chambers.

In spite of the Nazis' efforts to dehumanize our people, we maintained our values and traditions. Jewish religious practices were criminalized, but prayer services and holiday observances continued secretly, in hundreds of hidden sanctuaries.

At Passover, matzo was baked in secret underground kitchens. When wine was unavailable, seder cups were filled with the juice of raisins or beets.

In the face of the Nazis' efforts to destroy us, we remained true to ourselves and to each other, and to the ideals we care about, never giving up hope that the world would one day emerge from darkness.

The Nazis expected to eliminate the Warsaw Ghetto quickly and easily.

Instead, a starving, outnumbered, poorly armed, but powerful and determined Jewish resistance managed to fight back against the Nazis for forty-two days.

At one point the Jewish resistance was so ferocious that the Nazis temporarily retreated.

Eventually, they returned in greater numbers. But a few hundred Jews from the Warsaw Ghetto did manage to escape through the underground sewer lines, and joined anti-fascist groups in the woods and forests.

Similar acts of resistance took place in Minsk, Vilna, Bialystok, and other cities; and in the concentration camps, too, there were countless acts of resistance.

GROUP

We remember the heroism of the Jews —
men, women, and children —
who fought in the ghettos,
in the forests, on the war fronts,
together with all of democratic humanity,
to stop the curse of fascism
from engulfing the earth.

We will honor their memory
by dedicating ourselves to the cause
of peace and freedom in our land
and throughout the world.

THE GREAT SYNAGOGUE OF WARSAW
Completed in 1878; destroyed by the Nazis during the Warsaw Ghetto Uprising in 1943.

LEADER | GROUP

"Dayenu" is the name of a traditional Passover song that's over a thousand years old. Who can tell us what the word *dayenu* means?

"It would have been enough for us."

Yes! Very impressive.

It's actually not that impressive.
We just read it here in the book.

Let's sing a little bit of "Dayenu" in Hebrew. The chorus goes like this:

(All present who know the song can demonstrate the chorus.)

Da-dayenu, da-dayenu,
Da-dayenu, dayenu, dayenu!

If you don't want to sing,
you can still join in by banging on the table
or hitting a plate with a spoon.
Let's practice a nice, noisy chorus.

Da-dayenu, da-dayenu,
Da-dayenu, dayenu, dayenu!

Now, let's sing a couple of the original verses
and choruses in Hebrew.
Please sing along with the verse
or the chorus or both!

אִלּוּ הוֹצִיאָנוּ מִמִּצְרָיִם	*Ilu hotzi hotzianu,* *Hotzianu mimitzrayim,* *Hotzianu mimitzrayim,*
דַּיֵּנוּ	*Dayenu!*
	Da-dayenu, da-dayenu, *da-dayenu, dayenu, dayenu!*
אִלּוּ נָתַן לָנוּ אֶת הַשַּׁבָּת	*Ilu natan natan lanu,* *Natan lanu et hatorah,* *Natan lanu et hatorah,*
דַּיֵּנוּ	*Dayenu!*
	Da-dayenu, da-dayenu, *da-dayenu, dayenu, dayenu!*

LEADER

GROUP

In the traditional Haggadah, "Dayenu"
is a song of thanks to the ancient Hebrew god
for all the things he does for the Hebrews
in the original Exodus myth. For example,
the verses we just heard in Hebrew mean,
"Had he brought us out of Egypt,
and not given us the Torah..."

"It would have been enough for us."

Now let's bring "Dayenu" into the present
and out of the past perfect conditional.
We'll read around the table
and sing the chorus together.

When all people live free
from tyranny and oppression,
that will be enough for us.

Da-dayenu, da-dayenu,
da-dayenu, dayenu, dayenu!

When all people have access
to the resources necessary for survival,
that will be enough for us.

Da-dayenu, da-dayenu,
da-dayenu, dayenu, dayenu!

When all children are free to learn,
free from hunger, abuse, and neglect,
that will be enough for us.

Da-dayenu, da-dayenu,
da-dayenu, dayenu, dayenu!

When all people are free
to make their own reproductive decisions,
that will be enough for us.

Da-dayenu, da-dayenu,
da-dayenu, dayenu, dayenu!

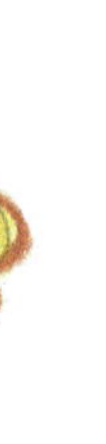

When our justice system is truly just
and no one is above the law,
that will be enough for us.

Da-dayenu, da-dayenu,
da-dayenu, dayenu, dayenu!

When all religions can be freely practiced or ignored,
and no religion can dictate public policy,
that will be enough for us.

Da-dayenu, da-dayenu,
da-dayenu, dayenu, dayenu!

When our political system effectively serves
the will of the people,
that will be enough for us.

Da-dayenu, da-dayenu,
da-dayenu, dayenu, dayenu!

When all people are free to experience
the love and happiness we feel tonight,
that will be enough for us.

Da-dayenu, da-dayenu,
da-dayenu, dayenu, dayenu!

LEADER

Now enough singing
and let's have dessert already!

LEADER

GROUP

So ends our Passover Haggadah.
But our conversation will continue.

We will always remember
the meaning of Passover —
the importance of remembering history,
the value of freedom, and our responsibility
as members of the human family
to oppose fascism and tyranny;
to care for one another;
to speak and listen openly.

Tonight, we renew these promises
to ourselves and to each other.

And tonight
is not different
from all other nights.

READ AROUND THE TABLE

The traditional Haggadah
ends with the phrase *Next year in Jerusalem.*
This was an expression of hope
for the future existence of a Jewish state
in the ancestral Jewish homeland, Israel.

Today, the modern state of Israel exists and thrives.
So we conclude our seder
by expressing another wish for the future.

Tonight, we've spoken
about freedom, safety, and security
for all people, everywhere.

Now we close
with a personal wish.

May every one of us
know not only liberty and safety,
but love and laughter and joy.

And so we say:

GROUP

***Next year,
wherever you
would most like to be.***

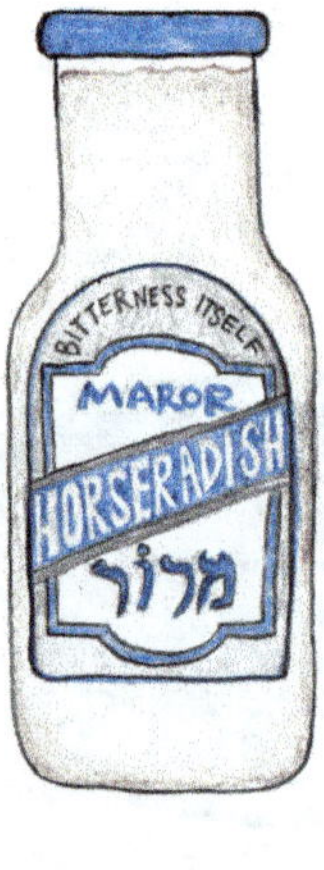
BITTERNESS ITSELF
MAROR
HORSERADISH
מרור

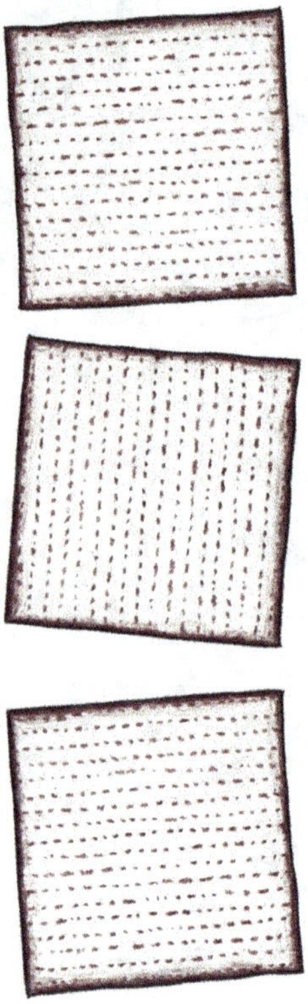

ABOUT THE AUTHOR

Noah Diamond is a writer, performer, designer, and producer whose works include *Pintele*, an audio series about Jewish identity, which inspired *The Pintele Haggadah.* His other projects include the multimedia monologue *400 Years in Manhattan* (and the book of the same title) and the comic strip saga *Love Marches On.* Noah restored and adapted the book and lyrics for the Marx Brothers' lost 1924 musical *I'll Say She Is*, and played the role of Groucho in the show's first-ever revival. Other Marx Brothers projects include the book *Gimme a Thrill: The Story of I'll Say She Is* and the "Freedonia trilogy" of streaming documentaries. He can be heard monthly as a cohost of *The Marx Brothers Council Podcast.* Noah lives in New York City with Amanda Sisk, his partner in life and art. Please visit noahdiamond.com.

www.ingramcontent.com/pod-product-compliance
Lightning Source LLC
LaVergne TN
LVHW081302100826
845148LV00005B/946

* 9 7 9 8 2 1 8 9 0 6 8 9 4 *